4/04

W9-CBR-390

A RIVER JOURNEY

The Yangtze

Rob Bowden

A RIVER JOURNEY

The Amazon The Ganges
The Mississippi The Nile
The Rhine The Yangtze

A River Journey: The Yangtze

Text copyright © 2004 Raintree
Series copyright © 2004 Raintree
Published by Raintree, a division of Reed Elsevier, Inc..

Copyright Permissions
Raintree
100 N. Lasalle, Suite 1200
Chicago, IL 60602.

Book Design: Jane Hawkins
Picture Research: Shelley Noronha, Glass Onion Pictures
Maps: Tony Fleetwood

Library of Congress Cataloging-in-Publication Data:
Cataloging-in-publication data is on file at the Library of Congress.

ISBN 0-7398-6074-7

Printed in Hong Kong.
1 2 3 4 5 6 7 8 9 0
08 07 06 05 04

The website addresses (URLs) included in this book were valid at the time of going to press. However, because of the nature of the Internet, it is possible that some addresses may have changed, or sites may have changed or closed down since publication. While the author and Publisher regret any inconvenience this may cause readers, no responsibility for any such changes can be accepted by either the author or the Publisher.

The maps in this book use a conical projection, and so the indicator for North on the main map is only approximate.

Picture Acknowledgments
Cover: James Davis Travel Photography; title page Malcolm Watson/ Still Pictures; contents Chris Catton/ Oxford Scientific Films; 5 & 13 (bottom) James Davis Travel Photography; 6 Ian Cumming/Tibet Images; 7 Josef Müller, www.Open-Eye-Photography.de; 8 Philip Reeve/ Eye Ubiquitous; 9 (top) Julia Waterlow/ Eye Ubiquitous; 9 (bottom) Nick Bonetti/ Eye Ubiquitous; 10 Rhodri Jones/ Panos Pictures; 11 Julio Etchart/ Still Pictures; 12 (top) Michael S. Yamashita/Corbis (bottom) Popperfoto; 13 Martyn Evans/ Travel Ink; 14 Mark Henley/ Panos Pictures; 15 Mark Henley/ Panos PicturesPage 16 Nathan Smith/ Sylvia Cordaiy Photo Library; 17 David Lansdown/ Sylvia Cordaiy Photo Library; 18 Mark Henley/ Panos Pictures; 19 Camera Press; 20 Tony Binns/ Easi-er; 21 (top) Malcolm Watson/ Still Pictures (bottom) James Davis Worldwide Photographic Travel Library; 22/23 Mark Henley/ Panos Pictures; 24 (main) Guy Marks/ Axiom (inset) Liu Liqun/Corbis; 25 Liu Liqun/Corbis; 26 Bobby Yip/ Reuters/ Popperfoto; 27 (right) Jiri Rezac/ Axiom (bottom) Johnathan Smith/ Sylvia Cordaiy Photo Library; 28 & 29 Johnathan Smith/ Sylvia Cordaiy Photo; 30 Benoit Gysembergh/ Camera Press; 31 (top) Zhang dunhua-Imagine China (inset right) Bobby Yip/ Reuters/ Popperfoto; 32 Edward Parker; 33 (top) Stephen Coyne/ Sylvia Cordaiy Photo Library; 33 (inset) Julio Etchart/ Still Pictures (bottom) Alain le Garsmeur/ Panos Pictures; 34 N. Durrell McKenne/ Hutchinson Library; 35 Chris Catton/ Oxford Scientific Films; 36 Roland Seitre/ Still Pictures; 37 Tony Binns/ Easi-er; 38 Richard Sharpley/ Hodder Wayland Picture Library; 39 (left) Tiziana and Gianni Baldizzone/Corbis (right) Gordon Clements/ Hodder Wayland Picture Library; 40 Robert Francis/ Hutchinson Library; 41 (left) Ric Ergenbright/Corbis (bottom) James Davis Worldwide Photographic Travel Library; 42 Catherine Platt/ Panos Pictures; 43 Earth Satellite Corporation/ Science Photo Library; 44/45 Mark Henley/ Impact

Contents

1. Mountains and Gorges 6

HISTORY	Mysterious source	7
NATURE	Fragile lands	7
ECONOMY	New opportunities	8
NATURE	Leap of faith	9
ECONOMY	Mountain farming	10
NATURE	Trees of life	11
PEOPLE	The Naxi of Lijiang	12
CHANGE	Rebuilding Lijiang	13

2. The Szechuan Basin 14

NATURE	Waters meet	15
PEOPLE	Crowded streets	15
ECONOMY	Industrial heartland	16
PEOPLE	Szechuan food	17
CHANGE	Rising waters	18
PEOPLE	Moving up!	19
ECONOMY	The Golden Waterway	20
NATURE	A dirty business	20

3. The Three Gorges 22

NATURE	The Three Gorges	23
ECONOMY	Gorge cruises	24
HISTORY	Yangtze dragons	25
HISTORY	Safe passage	25
CHANGE	Another Great Wall	26
NATURE	Sediment trap	27

4. The Yangtze Plains 28

ECONOMY	Ship staircase	29
NATURE	Plains and meanders	29
ECONOMY	Living with risk	30
PEOPLE	Drastic action	31
NATURE	The shrinking lake	32
ECONOMY	Transportation and textiles	32

5. Land of Fish and Rice 34

ECONOMY	Farming for fish	35
NATURE	Threatened Yangtze	36
HISTORY	Watering the land	37
ECONOMY	China's rice bowl	38
PEOPLE	Hard work!	38
HISTORY	Ancient capital	40
CHANGE	Grand Canal	41

6. The Yangtze Delta 42

NATURE	A watery world	43
PEOPLE	Vertical living	43
CHANGE	Into the future	44

FURTHER INFORMATION	46
GLOSSARY	47
INDEX	48

Your Guide to the River

USING THEMED TEXT As you make your journey down the Yangtze you will find topic headings about that area of the river. These symbols show what the text is about.

NATURE   Plants, wildlife, and the environment

HISTORY   Events and people in the past

PEOPLE   The lives and culture of local people

CHANGE   Things that have altered the area

$ ECONOMY   Jobs and industry in the area

USING MAP REFERENCES Each chapter has a map that shows the section of the river we are visiting. The numbered boxes show exactly where a place of interest is located.

SOURCE

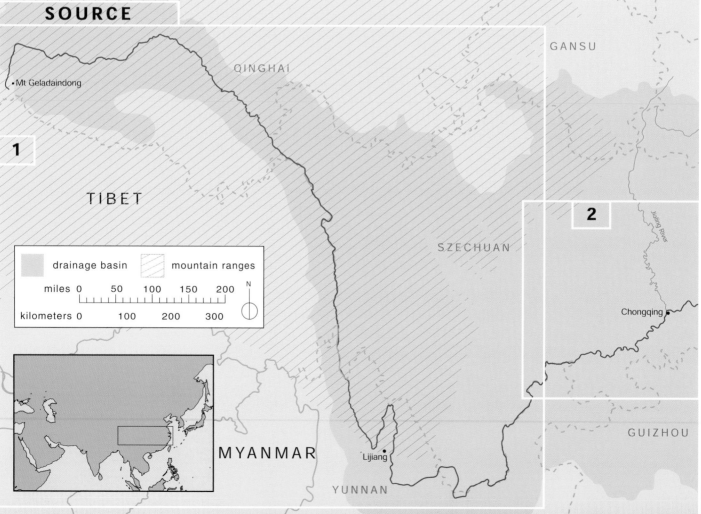

- drainage basin
- mountain ranges

miles 0   50   100   150   200   N

kilometers 0   100   200   300

The Journey Ahead

The Yangtze is Asia's longest river. In fact, its Chinese name Chang Jiang means "Long River." It is sometimes refered to as simply, the Chang. The Yangtze begins its 3,914-mi (6,300-km) journey high in the Qinghai-Tibet plateau of western China. After crossing the plateau, the river crashes over rapids and takes wild turns as it cascades 994 mi (1,600 km) through steep mountain valleys. At Yibin the Yangtze leaves the mountains. Several major tributaries join it as the Yangtze passes through the Szechuan basin.

Beyond Chongqing the river valley is wide enough to support several major settlements. However, it then narrows again at the dramatic Three Gorges. Past Yichang the Yangtze opens out into vast plains that stretch all the way to Nanjing. The delta beyond Nanjing is heavily urbanized, especially around Shanghai, just before the Yangtze ends its journey in the East China Sea.

Let's begin our river journey with a flight over the remote upper reaches of the Yangtze. We land at Lijiang and from there head by road into one of the world's deepest gorges.

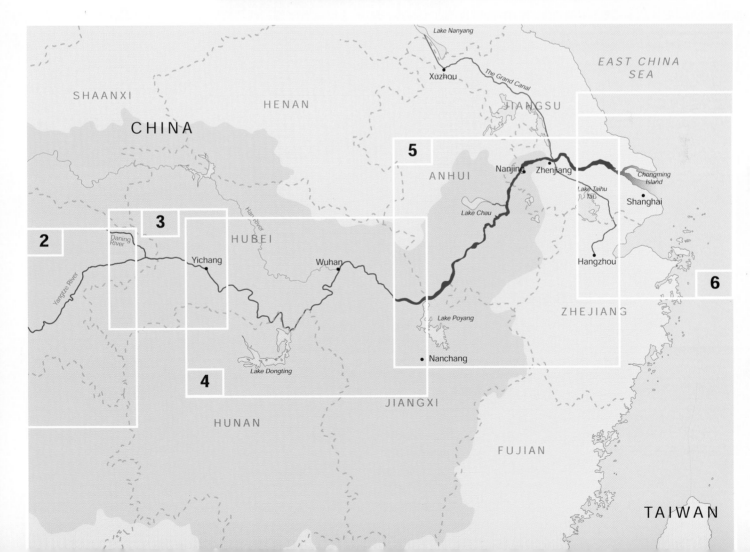

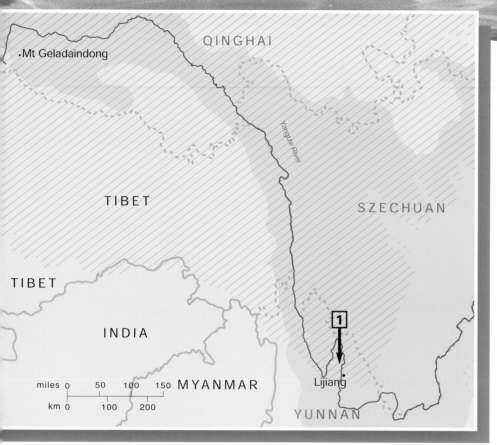

QINGHAI

·Mt Geladaindong

TIBET

Yangtze River

SZECHUAN

TIBET

INDIA

miles 0   50   100   150   MYANMAR

km 0   100   200

1

Lijiang

YUNNAN

1.*Mountains and Gorges*

FLYING OVER THE QINGHAI-TIBET plateau you can see how vast and isolated this region is. Our flight path follows the Yangtze for about 870 miles (1,400 kilometers) as it falls from its source into deep mountain valleys, almost disappearing from view at times. We land at Lijiang and take a bus trip along the steep roads to the spectacular Tiger Leaping Gorge. We learn about how people survive in this difficult environment, and then we return to Lijiang to experience the unique local culture.

Herders living on the vast Tibetan plateau mainly keep yaks. Their thick coats help the yaks withstand the bitter cold of winter.

Firewood is the main source of fuel for local people, but collecting it has had a dramatic impact on the environment.

📖 HISTORY *Mysterious source*

Finding the source of a river like the Yangtze is not an easy task. There are so many streams and rivers joining it that each one is a potential source. For many years, people believed the source to be the Min Jiang (*jiang* means "river" in Chinese). Then, in the mid-17th century, a Chinese geographer discovered that another river, the Jinsha, was even longer. Jinsha became the new name for the upper section of the Yangtze.

The true source of the Yangtze was still a mystery, however. Then, in 1976, a small glacier-fed lake called Qemo Lake at the foot of Mount Geladaindong, which is 21,519 feet (6,559 meters) high, was discovered. The lake was named as the source.

🐰 NATURE *Fragile lands*

The rainy season in the upper Yangtze is between April and August, and heavy storms are common during this period. Rainwater pours down mountain slopes and floods the plateau as it rushes to find the shortest route to the river. Because of the fragile land in this region, the surging rainwater erodes large amounts of soil. Human actions have made this problem even worse. Local people remove trees to use as fuel or for building, and livestock grazing removes the vegetation, leaving soils unprotected when it rains heavily.

In September 2001, the government announced a set of actions to reduce erosion in the upper Yangtze. The measures included educating people about soil conservation and improving local laws to protect the land from misuse. The government also plans to frequently monitor environmental protection in the upper Yangtze.

$ ECONOMY *New opportunities*

After flying over the Yangtze headwaters, we land at the airport in Lijiang. The airport opened in 1994. It has brought new opportunities and economic growth to this region.

Tourism has become big business around Lijiang, an ancient city famous for its narrow streets and traditional mountain culture. For us, as for many visitors, Lijiang is also the starting point for a visit to Tiger Leaping Gorge MAP REF: 1 . We take a bus to the gorge through the small town of Shigu located on the first major bend of the Yangtze. From Shigu the drive into the gorge is a thrilling adventure along a narrow road cut into the mountainside. There is

Few people live in the isolated mountain gorges of the upper Yangtze. We can see their villages from our plane.

only a small wall between our bus and the 655-foot (200-meter) drop to the valley below. The road was completed in 1997 as part of a plan to encourage tourism in Yunnan province.

As we make our final descent into Tiger Leaping Gorge, you can see that local people have taken advantage of the growth in tourism, too. The 1,000 steps between the viewpoint and the river's edge are lined with refreshment and souvenir stalls. There are even people who will carry you up the steps in a sedan chair if you get too tired.

NATURE *Leap of faith*

Tiger Leaping Gorge is one of the world's most spectacular natural sights. For 11 miles (17 kilometers) the Yangtze is squeezed between towering natural walls and it falls about 980 feet (300 meters) over eighteen sets of furious rapids. If you look up, you can see the gorge walls reaching for the sky above. In places they are over 9,800 feet (3,000 meters) high, making this one of the world's deepest gorges.

The gorge has been cut from the surrounding land by the force of the falling river water and the rocks and debris it carries. The rapids are formed where harder bands of rock cross the river bed and resist the force of the river. One of these harder rocks, Tiger Leaping Stone, sits above the water at a point where the gorge is just 98 feet (30 meters) wide. The stone and the gorge are named after a legend that tells of a tiger leaping across the gorge while being chased by hunters—a true leap of faith!

Right: The beauty of Tiger Leaping Gorge attracts many visitors. Below: The Yangtze crashes past tourists at Tiger Leaping Stone with incredible force.

$ ECONOMY *Mountain farming*

As we leave Tiger Leaping Gorge, we can see that a lot of the land in this area is farmed. Because there is so little flat land here, local farmers create their own by digging narrow terraces along the hillsides. This gives the local landscape its distinctive stepped appearance. Farmers remove stones from the plot and place them around its edges, which reduces soil erosion during heavy rain. If they need extra water, they connect small channels to the mountain streams that crisscross this area. Most of this work is done by hand, but on the larger plots farmers sometimes use water buffalo to plow the land before they plant it.

Farmers in this area grow a mixture of crops. They grow some, like corn, potatoes, and rice, for themselves. This is known as "subsistence farming." They grow other crops to sell; these are known as "cash crops." Cash crops in this region include sunflower seeds, which are grown for their oil. Tobacco is also grown here.

Farmers have become experts at building terraces into mountainsides in order to grow crops. This technique also reduces soil erosion.

NATURE *Trees of life*

Once the trees have been removed, steep slopes can quickly be eroded.

One of the problems with mountain farming is that people remove trees to create fields for farming as well as for fuel and building supplies. Trees are important because the canopy (the branches and leaves) protects the soil from the driving rain and the tree roots hold the soil together. When trees are removed, rain simply washes down the mountainsides, taking much of the soil with it. The soil is deposited in the Yangtze, adding to the natural sediment already carried by the river. The channel becomes shallower, which means that the river holds less water. There is then a much greater risk of flooding.

In 1998 the Yangtze experienced terrible flooding, the worst in 44 years. Deforestation was blamed because it had caused soil erosion in the upper reaches of the river. Since the 1950s, forests along the Yangtze have been reduced by half. Environmentalists have been warning for a long time that the clearing of trees would cause greater flooding of the Yangtze.

Finally, following the floods of 1998, the government acted. Strict new laws have now been introduced to reduce tree clearance, and local people are being educated about the importance of trees for flood control. Tree-planting projects have also been introduced to reduce erosion and rainwater runoff in some of the worst affected areas.

Above: The Naxi Orchestra has been in existence for hundreds of years. Left: A Dongba (holy man) writing in the Naxi's unique pictorial script.

✋ PEOPLE *The Naxi of Lijiang*

Few people live in the isolated mountainous environment of the upper Yangtze. One group that does, however, is the Naxi. Originally from Tibet, the Naxi have lived in the area around Lijiang for more than 1,000 years. Today there are about 250,000 Naxi people. They grow crops like rice and wheat, and they also breed horses that are regarded as some of the strongest in China. In recent years, the Naxi have become involved in tourism as visitors from China and abroad come to learn more about their unique culture.

The Naxi religion is known as "Dongba," named after the shamans, or holy men, who teach and preserve its traditions. Dongba religion is centered on the belief that all natural things have a soul. The Naxi worship the sun and moon, the clouds and mountains, and, of course, the Yangtze itself. Today, the

Above: Lijiang is being rebuilt following a major earthquake in 1996. Money from increased tourism in China is helping to fund the rebuilding.

Dongba spend many hours translating ancient scripts that experts believe date back to the 900s. Their writing is actually a series of pictures instead of letters. Writing like this is known as pictorial script. The Naxi are thought to be the last people in the world to still use pictorial script.

Music is also a big part of Naxi culture, The famous Naxi Orchestra is said to have started in the 1200s when a great emperor named Kublai Khan donated instruments to the Naxi after they helped his army cross the Yangtze. Most of the instruments are either strummed or hammered and produce beautiful, haunting sounds.

➡ CHANGE *Rebuilding Lijiang*

On February 3,1996, the Lijiang area suffered a major earthquake. Over 250 people were killed and more than 4,000 were seriously injured. In Lijiang itself, about a third of the town was destroyed, including some of its oldest buildings. As the area is rebuilt, the Chinese government is encouraging its development as a major tourist center. It believes that the combination of the spectacular Yangtze gorges and the fascinating Naxi culture will make Lijiang a key center for China's rapidly growing tourist industry.

They may be right, but others are concerned that developing the area for tourism may spoil its charms and turn the Naxi people into little more than a living tourist exhibition.

We take off from Lijiang and follow the Yangtze out of the mountains and across the Szechuan basin beyond Yibin. We land in Chongqing where we can finally take to the river.

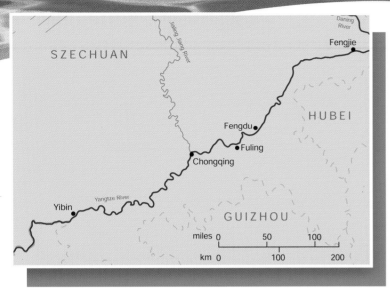

2. The Szechuan Basin

AS WE LAND IN CHONGQING, we have already followed the Yangtze for about two-thirds of its journey. It is at Chongqing, however, that the river really comes to life. We spend some time exploring this bustling city, and we sample some of the local food. The port is the center of Chongqing's economy, and we discover the importance of the Yangtze for trade in this part of China. As we continue our journey toward Fengjie, we pass through an area that will soon be flooded by a major dam being built downstream. We consider the changes this will mean for people living here and the problems it may cause.

The view from one of the cable cars that carry people between the mainland and the peninsula shows just how fast Chongqing is growing.

The steep and crowded path to Chaotianmen Docks. Balancing cargo on these poles is a skill that takes years to master.

🐰 NATURE *Waters meet*

Chongqing marks a major change in the Yangtze. The river is slower and has widened since leaving the narrow mountain gorges. Several tributaries join the Yangtze as it approaches the city. In Chongqing itself, the Yangtze is joined by the Jialing River, which began life about 450 miles (720 kilometers) to the north. The hilly peninsula of land between the confluence of the two rivers is the commercial center of Chongqing. As the population has grown, however, the city has spread beyond the peninsula onto the land beyond both the Yangtze and Jialing Rivers. One of the most interesting ways to travel between the peninsula and the mainland is by cable car. There are two cable cars, one across each river, and they both give fantastic views of this thriving river city.

✋ PEOPLE *Crowded streets*

Chongqing has been the most important city in southwestern China for many years. Its continued importance to modern China was made clear in 1997 when it was separated from Szechuan province and made into its own municipality. Chongqing is also the most populated city in southwestern China. It was home to nearly 6 million people in 2002. An additional 24 million live in the municipal area, many of them in the towns and villages that line the Yangtze and Jialing Rivers.

With so many people, the streets of Chongqing are extremely crowded, especially around the docks. Because the streets are so steep, there are no bicycles—the normal way to transport goods in Chinese cities. It's an unusual sight for us to see people carrying things in baskets slung from poles balanced across their shoulders. It takes some skill to navigate the narrow streets.

Chongqing has become a center for vehicle production in China. The Yangtze is a vital route for transporting finished goods to the rest of China.

$ ECONOMY *Industrial heartland*

Chongqing is an area rich in natural resources. It has China's biggest reserves of natural gas. It also has large quantities of coal, rock salt, and precious metals, including mercury and manganese. This reason, together with the city's position on the banks of the Yangtze, makes Chongqing an ideal location for an industrial city. From here raw materials and finished goods can be transported to Shanghai and the East China Sea. Because the area is mountainous, without the Yangtze transportation would be difficult.

The center of activity in Chongqing is Chaotianmen Docks. From here, millions of tons of cargo are moved up and down the river, or sent to the railroads and highways that link Chongqing to other parts of western China.

Many of Chongqing's main industries are based on its natural resources. Since the mid 1980s, however, manufacturing has also become important. Vehicle production has been particularly successful. By the late 1990s, Chongqing's factories were producing more than 1,900,000 cars and other vehicles a year. The success of Chongqing's industries is evident from the rapid growth of the city. Look at the huge cranes dotting the landscape. Each new building seems bigger than the last, reaching ever higher into the sky. There is a downside to this success, however. Emissions from factories and traffic cause high levels of air pollution. Chongqing is often covered in a persistent, choking haze. Pollution from Chongqing also affects the Yangtze, as we'll soon see.

✋ PEOPLE *Szechuan food*

Before leaving Chongqing, we must sample the local Szechuan cooking. One of the main ingredients in Szechuan cooking is chili pepper and many of the most popular dishes are hot and spicy. Chicken, duck, fish, pork, vegetables, and rice are all found on the menu. There are also more unusual items such as braised frog and snake. The speciality, though, is Szechuan hotpot, known locally as *huoguo*. Diners cook meat and vegetables at their table in a bubbling pot of spiced chicken stock. Once cooked, the food is flavored with spicy oil, salt, and chili powder. Hotpot originated in Chongqing and is found in most of the open-air cafés where people gather to talk and eat. Sitting in one of Chongqing's cafés is a great way to meet local people.

Szechuan hotpot is a local speciality. Cooking and eating it together is a great social occasion.

→ CHANGE *Rising waters*

A cable railroad takes us down to the muddy riverbanks and the passenger ferry that will carry us downstream to Fengjie. As the ferry sets off, the strong current swiftly carries us away. Looking back you can see how Chongqing is preparing itself for the effects of rising waters in this part of the Yangtze. New roads are being built high above the current river level, and new buildings are now growing upward instead of outward across land that will soon be flooded. High on the riverbanks new flood defenses give some idea of how much water levels could rise.

Water levels are rising because by 2009 this area will become part of the world's biggest reservoir. The reservoir will stretch 455 miles (632 kilometers) downstream from Chongqing to the enormous Three Gorges Dam being built at Sandouping. We visit the dam later in our journey, but it is in this area of the Yangtze that many of dam's effects will be felt. Water levels are expected to rise by up to 328 feet (100 meters) behind the dam wall. They will permanently flood any land below this new waterline. The Yangtze between Chongqing and Sandouping

Shibaozhai pagoda is known as the "Pearl of the Three Gorges." When the Three Gorges Dam is complete, the water will totally submerge these houses below it.

will be changed forever, and much of what we see on this stretch of the journey may be underwater in a few years' time.

$ PEOPLE *Moving up!*

The rising waters of the Three Gorges reservoir will not only flood land. They will also flood more than 1,300 villages, 326 towns, and 19 cities along this stretch of the Yangtze. To protect these communities from the rising waters, China is now moving up to 1.9 million people to new settlements above the waterline. This is one of the biggest resettlement programs the world has ever seen. Resettlement began in 1997 and will continue until the dam is finished in 2009. In some parts of the river, settlements are moving to higher ground, as we saw in Chongqing. In other areas, whole towns and villages have been completely relocated.

Despite financial help from the government, many people are unhappy about being moved from their homes. Many have lived in them all their lives. The Chinese of this area believe in worshiping their ancestors. To watch their ancestral homes disappear underwater is especially difficult.

These villagers have to relocate because their villages will soon be underwater. Not everyone is happy to move.

$ ECONOMY The Golden Waterway

Seventy percent of water transportation in China is on the Yangtze, and 80 percent of all the cargo transported by river is on the Yangtze. The river's importance to the Chinese economy has earned it the name of the "Golden Waterway." However, between Chongqing and Yichang, which is downstream of the new reservoir, the Yangtze's waters are too shallow for larger trade vessels to navigate. This is because the riverbed has numerous areas of sand or gravel that build up and reduce the depth of the river. These areas are known as shoals.

Soon, however, the shoals will be a problem of the past. The new reservoir behind the Three Gorges Dam will increase the water depth dramatically. Large oceangoing vessels, ten times the size of current ones, will be able to navigate the complete waterway between Chongqing and the East China Sea. The improvements in navigation are expected to increase river traffic on the Golden Waterway by up to five times and reduce the cost of shipping by about a third. This will bring new trade and wealth to the people living along the Yangtze and especially around major ports such as Chongqing.

🐇 NATURE A dirty business

Although the Yangtze is vital to the Chinese economy, many of the activities that take place along its banks are extremely dirty. The heavy industries you can see, such as

When the Three Gorges Dam is complete, vessels up to ten times the size of these will be able to safely travel along the Yangtze.

steel and chemical factories, produce large quantities of waste. Agriculture is not much better. Fertilizers and pesticides used on the fields spread into the wider environment. A lot of this pollution finds its way into the Yangtze, which has major impacts on the river.

In January 2002 one study estimated that more than 6.5 million tons of garbage and almost 11 million tons of industrial solid waste were being dumped into the upper Yangtze every year. If liquid waste from homes, sewers, and industries is included, the figures are even higher. Chongqing alone spews over a billion tons of waste water into the Yangtze every year, 90 percent of it from industrial sources. The government has been trying to clean up the Yangtze by spending $4.8 billion on waste controls from 2002 to 2012. Though this is welcomed, some fear it may be too little too late.

Our ferry calls at the port town of Fuling and passes Fengdu before arriving in Fengjie. We transfer to a tourist cruise ship for our journey to the Three Gorges.

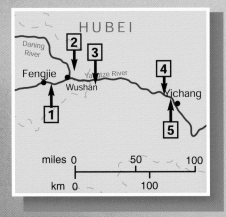

3. The Three Gorges

FENGJIE IS A SMALL, BUSY TOWN at one end of the Yangtze's famous Three Gorges. We join other tourists on board one of the many cruise ships heading downstream to Yichang. The water here is already beginning to rise, but the Three Gorges are still a breathtaking sight. At the end of the first gorge in Wushan, we take a short diversion along the Daning River to explore the beautiful Lesser Three Gorges. Back on the Yangtze we reach the construction site of the new dam at Sandouping as we leave the last of the Three Gorges. We can't stop at the site for the new dam because it is a restricted area, so we continue toward Yichang, passing through the smaller Gezhou Dam on the way.

The stunning beauty and dramatic scale of the entrance to Qutang Gorge has enchanted travelers for centuries.

The Three Gorges

The Three Gorges were formed by a vast inland sea that carved its way through a series of faults in the earth's surface. This all took place about 70 million years ago. The dramatic results are all around us as we zigzag our way through the limestone gorges for the next 80 miles (129 kilometers). Sections of the gorge stretch above us, rising as jagged peaks up to 3,900 feet (1,200 meters) high. In places the rocks have formed into strange shapes, many of which have been given interesting names. In Xiling Gorge, for example, you will find rocks named Ox Liver, Horse Lung, and Sword. The steepest slopes have no vegetation on them, but the lower slopes are covered in forests or grassland.

As the Yangtze passes through the Three Gorges, it collects water and sediment from several small tributaries.

In places the tributaries have cut deep ravines in the walls of the gorge, and in millions of years they could become gorges in their own right. Many of the smaller tributaries will be flooded as this part of the river rises behind the Three Gorges Dam downstream. White markers high on the valley sides indicate the level the water is expected to reach. Other markers indicate the height of previous floods. One of the main reasons the dam is being built is to prevent flooding, as we will soon discover.

$ ECONOMY _Gorge cruises_

Like us, most visitors see the Three Gorges by taking a cruise along the Yangtze. Some of the boats are extremely luxurious and travel nonstop between Chongqing and Wuhan, downstream of the Three Gorges. As travel to China becomes easier, the country is expected to become the world's number one tourist destination by 2020. The Three Gorges will be one of its top attractions, and several tour companies have already ordered new boats to meet the demand.

The first gorge we see as we head downstream is the impressive Qutang Gorge MAP REF: 1 . It may be the shortest gorge, at just 5 miles (8 kilometers) long, but its near vertical mountainsides provide a grand entrance to the gorges. High up on one side is an old towpath that was once used to tow boats through the gorge before navigation was improved. At the end of Qutang Gorge, we moor at Wushan and take a short diversion along the Daning River to visit the Lesser Three Gorges MAP REF: 2 . Though lesser by name, they are equally, if not more, spectacular. Many visitors rate them as the highlight of a Yangtze cruise.

📖 HISTORY *Yangtze dragons*

Back on the Yangtze, we continue into Wu Gorge MAP REF: 3 , famous for its Yangtze river dragons. Legend has it that twelve wild dragons created chaos in the river and its gorge, leading to floods and destruction wherever they went. Yao Ji, a daughter of the Queen Mother of the West, defeated the dragons and then turned herself and her eleven sisters into twelve peaks (six on each side of the gorge) to safely guide boats and protect local villagers. Many other myths and legends are told about the Three Gorges, but the story of Yao Ji is one of the best known. As we pass through Wu Gorge, you may spot Goddess Peak, said to be Yao Ji herself in the shape of a kneeling maiden.

📖 HISTORY *Safe passage*

The final gorge, Xiling MAP REF: 4 , is also the longest at 47 miles (76 kilometers). In the past, it was also the most dangerous of the gorges, and countless travelers drowned in its turbulent and rocky waters. Then in the 1950s, the government improved navigation by using dynamite to blast away the dangerous rocks, creating a safe passage for boats. Today we follow other river traffic in a convoy between markers showing the safest route.

Left: Tourists look ahead as they approach the entrance to Qutang gorge. Left inset: Many of The Three Gorges cruise boats are like floating hotels, carrying up to 260 passengers. The new ones will be even bigger. Right: Local legends on how Wu Gorge was formed focus on its dramatic rock formations.

CHANGE *Another Great Wall*

The Great Wall of China is the country's most famous landmark, but it will soon be joined by another Great Wall, this one across the Yangtze. As we leave Xiling Gorge, we see the "wall" for the first time—the Three Gorges Dam, being built at the town of Sandouping MAP REF: 5 . When it is finished in 2009, it will stretch 1.2 miles (two kilometers) across the Yangtze and stand 607 feet (185 meters) high—as high as a 45-story office building.

Since the start of the dam's construction in 1994, there has been a lot of argument about it. Supporters of the dam say that it will control flooding on the Yangtze. During the 20th century, floods killed more than 320,000 people, 4,000 of them during the last serious floods in 1998. The dam will also generate hydroelectric power (HEP) for China's growing energy needs. It will provide the equivalent of 18 nuclear power stations or the burning of 44 million tons (40 million metric tons) of coal a year. Those against the dam say that building it will damage the environment and disrupt the lives of local people. It will also cause the destruction of shrines and other artifacts of historical importance. They believe a series of smaller dams would have less impact. They are particularly worried about what might happen if the

> The model and artist's drawing help people to understand what the Three Gorges Dam will look like when it is finished in 2009.

dam were ever damaged by a major flood or earthquake. When finished, the dam will be the biggest in the world. As we pass the site, you will see some of the 30,000 workers, 40 cranes, and hundreds of trucks involved in this amazing and controversial project.

NATURE *Sediment trap*

The Yangtze carries 550 to 770 million tons (500 to 700 million metric tons) of sediment downstream every year, the fourth biggest load of all the world's rivers. Normally, sediment is deposited along the length of the river or washed out to sea. Some experts are concerned, however, that the new dam could become a giant sediment trap, reducing the depth of the river and causing greater flooding as far upstream as Chongqing. Shipping would also be affected and, in the worst case, the buildup of sediment and rising waters could turn the Three Gorges Dam into a giant waterfall.

Engineers have built a series of 23 sluice gates in the dam wall to flush the sediment downstream, but no one is sure if such gates will work because they've never been used on a river with so much sediment.

Our journey downstream is blocked by another dam, the Gezhou. To pass below it, we enter a ship lock.

miles 0   50   100

km 0   100   200

HUBEI

Han River

Yangtze River

Yichang

Wuhan

1

2

HUNAN

JIANGXI

Lake Dongting

4. *The Yangtze Plains*

AFTER NAVIGATING THE ship lock through the Gezhou Dam, our cruise ship leaves us in Yichang. We catch another passenger ferry to take us farther downstream. The Yangtze is slowing now and becomes almost sluggish as it meanders through the low, flat land of the Yangtze Plains. Flooding is a big threat in this region, and people have to combat it. A short diversion takes us to Lake Dongting, China's second largest lake. In the industrial city of Wuhan, we visit a textile factory.

The landscape below the Gezhou Dam is much flatter, and the river begins to slowly meander around enormous bends.

$ ECONOMY *Ship staircase*

The Gezhou Dam MAP REF: 1 is 1.6 miles (2.6 kilometers) wide and 230 feet (70 meters) high. To pass below it, we enter one of three ship locks, two of which are among the biggest in the world. They can lower or raise ships of up to 11,000 tons (10,000 metric tons). The locks are vital to navigation on the Yangtze and to the growth of the economy in this region. Similar ship locks are now being built at the Three Gorges Dam upstream. When it is completed, this section of the Yangtze will become one of the most advanced shipping passages in the world—a sort of giant ship staircase.

Going downstream, we enter the lock at the level of the river above the Gezhou dam. The enormous doors close behind us, and the water in the lock chamber is slowly released. After just over an hour, we reach

The ship locks in the Gezhou Dam are huge. Navigating them is a memorable event for tourists enjoying a Yangtze river cruise.

the level of the river below the dam. The doors finally open. We dock in Yichang, an important transportation center on this part of the Yangtze.

NATURE *Plains and meanders*

As our ferry leaves Yichang, the landscape changes dramatically. We are entering the Yangtze floodplain, an enormous area of flat, low-lying land. The floodplain has been built up over hundreds of thousands of years as the Yangtze has deposited sediment onto the surrounding land during its annual flooding. The river slows as sediment builds up, and it begins to wind its way across the floodplain in a series of bends called meanders. In places, old meanders are cut off from the main channel and form isolated patches of water known as oxbow lakes.

Living with risk

The sediment of the floodplain is very rich in nutrients and makes extremely fertile farmland. You can see more farming here than at any point on our journey so far. The millions of people living here, however, also live with the risk of flooding. If the Yangtze rises too high, then it naturally spills onto the surrounding floodplain as it has for thousands of years. With so many people now living and farming on this land, there is a constant battle between them and the Yangtze. There are many examples where the Yangtze seems to be winning this battle. In 1998, for example, the Yangtze flooded about 487 acres of farmland an area equivalent to about 443 football fields.

The fertile floodplains provide rich farmland, but they can also ruin farmers when the land floods after a period of heavy rain.

But people in this area have been fighting back for hundreds of years. One example of their struggle is the 113-mile (182-kilometer) Jingjiang levee **MAP REF: 2**, which was started in 345 C.E.—over 1,650 years ago. The levee is a wall of earth along the bank of the river that protects eight million people, two major cities, and nearly 2 million acres of farmland. As we journey down the Yangtze, you will see many more levees protecting the people of the floodplains. In fact there are now 2,240 miles (3,600 kilometers) of major levees and 18,640 miles (30,000 kilometers) of smaller ones along the Yangtze.

Above: In 1999 the army and volunteers struggled to mend a burst levee protecting the city of Jingjiang.
Right: Boats were more useful than cars on the streets of Jiujiang following the floods of 1998.

✋ PEOPLE *Drastic action*

Although levees are built to protect people and their land, in serious floods they can sometimes break. If this happens suddenly, it can have dramatic consequences. A wall of water rushes across the low-lying land below. During the 1998 floods, levees in various sections of the river gave way and caused massive damage. The city of Jiujiang (downstream of Wuhan) was badly affected when a 131-foot (40-meter) gap opened up in the levee protecting it. The Yangtze poured through, flooding the homes of 40,000 people with almost 6.5 feet (2 meters) of water.

To avoid similar damage elsewhere, the government decided to take drastic action.

It removed about 330,000 people from their homes in the upper Yangtze so that nearby levees could be broken and the land flooded. Although severe, this action reduced the risk of flooding in the heavily populated and important industrial areas of the middle and lower Yangtze.

NATURE *The shrinking lake*

About two miles downstream of the Jingjiang levee we reach Lake Dongting. It is the second largest lake in China, covering about 1,060 square miles (2,740 square kilometers)—almost twice the area of Los Angeles. One hundred and fifty years ago, however, Lake Dongting was double that size.

Over the years, the Yangtze's floodwaters have been pushed downstream by the Jingjiang levee instead of flooding onto the surrounding plains. As the waters arrive at Lake Dongting, they slow and deposit the sediment they are carrying. Over the years the deposits have caused the lake to gradually silt up. Farmers in this region have made the problem worse. They have built small dikes around the edge of the lake to reclaim land as the water evaporates. In 1999 the government announced that farmers should break down some of these dikes. This would help store water during serious floods as part of China's national flood prevention plan.

$ ECONOMY *Transportation and textiles*

When we reach Wuhan, the Yangtze is joined by its longest tributary, the Han River. The Han rises 960 miles (1,540 kilometers) to the northwest (above Chongqing on our main map, pages 4-5).

Wuhan itself is a major transportation center and provides links between the river, road, and rail networks. You can see how lively the streets are with the bustle of

Land reclaimed for farming has contributed to a fall in Lake Dongting's water levels.

Above: This road-and-rail bridge across the Yangtze has increased Wuhan's importance as a transportation center.

Right: Thousands of people, especially women, are employed in Wuhan's textile industries.

people and goods transferring between different forms of transportation. At one time the only way to cross the Yangtze at this point, where it is 4, 920 feet (1,500 meters) wide, was by ferry. Even rail traffic was taken across by ferry until 1957 when a bridge was built across the Yangtze. A second bridge was completed in 1995. Today Wuhan provides the vital north-south rail link across the Yangtze, connecting Beijing (the Chinese capital) in the north to Guangzhou and Hong Kong in the south.

Wuhan's good transportation links and its location in one of China's main cotton-growing regions make Wuhan a natural center for the textile industry. Wuhan's factories export fabric and clothes all over the world. China is one of the world's biggest producers of textiles. In 2001 China exported textiles worth over $53 billion, 20 percent of all China's export earnings. Wuhan is also an industrial city with iron and steel works, vehicle production, and shipbuilding.

We leave Wuhan on one of the many grain barges heading downstream into one of China's most important farming regions.

5. Land of Fish and Rice

DOWNSTREAM OF WUHAN, we enter the "Land of Fish and Rice." As the name suggests, farming and fishing are very important here. In fact, the area between here and the Yangtze delta produces about 70 percent of China's paddy rice, 40 percent of its grain, and over half of its freshwater fish catch. We'll learn more about rice farming and fishing and look at the impact fishing has had on wildlife in the Yangtze. Nanjing, the ancient capital of China, is our next stop. Then we leave our barge when the Yangtze meets the Grand Canal at Zhenjiang.

Below: This farmer is feeding fish kept in special ponds. Fish farming, or aquaculture, is an ancient but fast-growing practice in China.

$ ECONOMY *Farming for fish*

Fishing is an important activity along this stretch of the Yangtze and in the numerous lakes, such as Poyang and Chao, found nearby. In 1998 Chinese fishers caught almost 2.5 million tons (2.3 million metric tons) of freshwater fish, which was 28.5 percent of the world total. This was the biggest catch of any country in the world, and over half of it came from the Yangtze.

Various fishing methods are used on the river, but one of the more unusual is the use of tamed cormorants. Cormorants are expert fish-catching birds. They dive from the edge of fishing boats to catch the fish underwater. They are prevented from swallowing the fish by a ring placed around their necks.

China also leads the world in fish farming, or aquaculture. In 1998 it produced nearly 30 million tons (27 million metric tons) of fish. Although part of this was

Fishing with the help of cormorants is an unusual fishing technique that has survived through generations of change.

exported, much was eaten locally. In fact, the average Chinese person eats more than 37 pounds (17 kilograms) of farmed fish every year. This compares with just 4.6 pounds (2.1 kilograms) per person per year in the rest of the world.

You may have noticed that many farmers keep fish ponds on their land. This is partly to earn money, but the ponds have other uses, too. They supply water for crops and their sediment provides a rich, natural fertilizer for the fields. In turn, farm waste is added to the ponds to encourage the growth of algae, plankton, and plants that the fish feed on. This simple and sustainable system has been practiced here for about 5,000 years.

 **NATURE** *Threatened Yangtze*

Fish stocks and other wildlife of the Yangtze are today under threat. The increase in fishing is one of the causes, but an increase in river traffic and pollution are also to blame. A clear sign of the problem has been the fall in the commercial fish catch on the Yangtze. In 1954, 478,000 tons (434,000 metric tons) were caught, but by 2002 this had fallen to less than half that amount. In response the government introduced its first-ever ban on commercial fishing, between February and May, the months when the fish under threat are breeding.

The most endangered species on the Yangtze is the baiji river dolphin. This unique mammal, related to the whale, is

The baiji, or Chinese river dolphin, is endangered. Being caught in fishing nets or hit by boats are the main reasons for its decline.

thought to have lived in the river for over 70 million years. The number of baiji in the Yangtze has fallen from more than 6,000 in the 1950s to fewer than 300 today. About half the baiji have died by getting tangled in fishing nets and drowning (river dolphins need to come up for air to breathe). A further third have been killed by collisions with boats and their propellers. The remaining baiji find it difficult to survive in the polluted waters of the Yangtze.

HISTORY *Watering the land*

Quite a lot of the farmland around us is artificially watered, or irrigated, using water from the Yangtze and its lakes and tributaries. Irrigation in China can be traced back about 4,000 years. Many of the methods used have hardly changed and can still be seen today.

For example, surface irrigation, or flooding the land from channels dug into the earth, still accounts for 99 percent of all irrigated farmland in China. Nearly half of this land is used for growing rice, the same crop for which irrigation was first developed all those years ago.

Since 1949 the use of electric or diesel pumps to lift water from rivers and lakes has dramatically increased the amount of irrigated farmland. In fact, by 2000, the area of irrigated land had increased threefold to an amazing 126 million acres (51 million hectares)—just over half of all China's farmland.

As the demand for food increases, irrigation will continue to expand. By 2050 the area of irrigated farmland is expected to be nearly the size of Texas.

A farmer uses a water-raising device to irrigate his fields. An abandoned waterwheel (in the background) is another traditional method of lifting water.

Transplanting rice from the nursery beds to the paddy fields is back-breaking work. The wide hat provides protection from the sun.

$ ECONOMY *China's rice bowl*

Rice is the staple crop in China and is eaten by almost everyone on a daily basis. There are two main types of rice grown in China—upland rice and wet, or paddy, rice. Upland rice grows like most other grains, but wet rice, as its name suggests, grows level fields, known as paddies, that are flooded with water. Rainfall provides some water, but most comes from irrigation systems like those we have seen along the Yangtze. In China, nearly all paddy rice is dependent on irrigation. Water is drained or pumped from rivers or lakes and distributed to the paddies through a system of channels. When it gets to the paddy, the water floods onto the land through an opening or gate in the irrigation channel. In some areas, lifting devices such as waterwheels or scoops are also used to apply the water.

You can see paddy rice growing all around us in this region. In fact, China produces about a third of the world's paddy rice. The plentiful water and warm temperatures make this area so good for rice farming that it is often known as "the rice bowl of China."

PEOPLE *Hard work*

Growing rice is extremely hard work and has not changed very much in the past 2,000 years. Farmers sow the rice in a nursery field before transplanting it to a shallow, flooded paddy after four or five weeks. Small earthen walls called bunds are built around the edge of the paddy to contain the water. Farmers increase the depth of the water as the rice grows—normally it reaches a depth of 4 to 6 inches (10 to 15 centimeters). As the rice grows, it needs regular weeding, and farmers may apply chemicals to help reduce weeds and pests. After ten to twelve weeks, the rice begins to turn golden, and the farmers

Above: Most Chinese people eat a bowl of rice every day. Right: Chinese farmers produce a wide variety of vegetables and sell them at local markets.

break the bunds to drain the paddy.

The rice is then ready to be harvested, threshed, and stored, an event that often involves the whole family. Finally, the stalks are dug or plowed back into the ground using water buffalo, ready for the whole cycle to start again. In this area, farmers sometimes grow two rice crops a year. In the cooler winter months, they grow wheat or other crops.

Ancient capital

As we approach the ancient city of Nanjing, we see buildings and industry instead of rice paddies. Nanjing means "southern capital" and true to its name, the city has been China's capital at various times in its five-or six-thousand-year history. In fact, the city you see around you has been the capital of ten kingdoms, or dynasties as they are known in China, since 229 C.E. Nanjing was also the capital of the Republic of China from 1911-1949. When the communist government took control of mainland China in 1949, Beijing became the capital of the People's Republic of China.

One of the most striking features of Nanjing is the impressive city walls. They were originally built about 2,500 years ago. The walls you can see today date back to 1369 when they were strengthened by the first emperor of the Ming dynasty. The walls now stretch an amazing 20 miles (32 kilometers) around the city, making them the longest city walls in the world.

The city attracts many tourists from China and abroad. Most come to see the famous walls, but others come to visit the burial place of Sun Yat-sen, an important national hero and the man who founded modern China in 1911.

The mausoleum of Sun Yat-sen is a popular attraction in China's ancient capital, Nanjing.

→ CHANGE *Grand Canal*

Around 50 miles (80 kilometers) downstream of Nanjing, we come face to face with China's other great inland waterway, the Grand Canal at the city of Zhenjiang MAP REF: 1. The canal crosses the Yangtze and runs between Beijing in the north and Hangzhou in the south. At 1,118 miles (1,800 kilometers), the Grand Canal is the world's longest human-made waterway. Parts of it are 2,400 years old.

The canal is still a major transportation route for grain and other goods. Our grain barge leaves us here and joins others as they travel nose to tail up the canal like a giant, mechanical river serpent. Barges cannot currently travel the entire length of the canal because of a buildup of sediment. To tackle this problem, water engineers plan to divert water from the Yangtze to raise the level in the canal. Dredging will remove sediment from the worst sections.

In 2000 plans were also announced to extend the canal south of Hangzhou to the port of Ningbo. This is part of the government's hopes to restore the Grand Canal to its former glory.

Boats travel in convoys along the narrow waterways of the Grand Canal, the longest canal in the world.

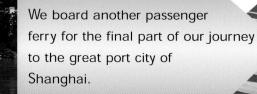

We board another passenger ferry for the final part of our journey to the great port city of Shanghai.

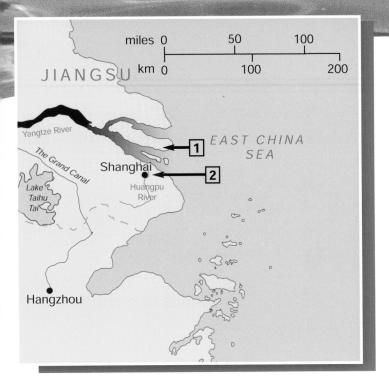

JIANGSU

miles 0   50   100

km 0   100   200

Yangtze River

The Grand Canal

Lake Taihu Tai

Shanghai

Hangzhou

Huangpu River

EAST CHINA SEA

1

2

6. *The Yangtze Delta*

WE ARE NOW IN THE VAST Yangtze delta where the river slows and widens in the final stages of its journey. The delta has long been important as a major trading center, providing the link between the Yangtze and the East China Sea, and beyond that, the Pacific Ocean. Shanghai, one of China's largest cities, is located at the mouth of the Yangtze, but the whole delta region is densely populated. As China's economy grows, the delta is becoming heavily developed and will play a key role in China's future.

Shanghai's bustling modern streets are a sharp contrast to the rural areas we have traveled through.

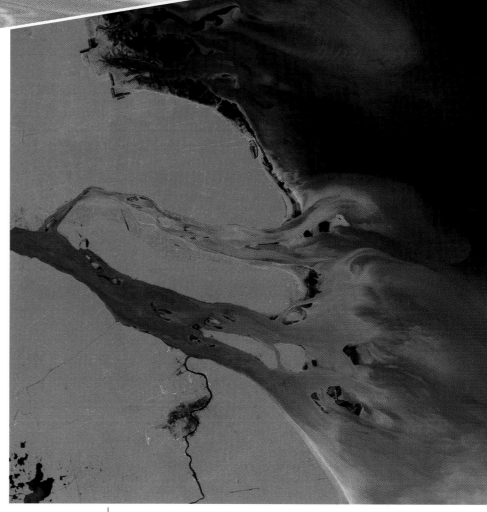

🐇 NATURE *A watery world*

Deltas are formed as a river slows and deposits its sediment at a rate faster than the sea or ocean is able to carry it away. Over millions of years, the Yangtze delta has built up into a vast, flat area, crossed by numerous streams and river channels as water struggles to find its way to the sea. The Yangtze widens dramatically in the delta and reaches a width of about 50 miles (80 kilometers) at its mouth.

In the mouth of the Yangtze lies Chongming Island MAP REF: 1, the largest of several islands found in the Yangtze delta. The island is formed entirely by the deposit of sediment over the years, and it splits the Yangtze into two channels for its final journey to the sea. We stick to the southern channel as we head through the watery world of the delta toward the teeming city of Shanghai.

🖐 PEOPLE *Vertical living*

The Yangtze delta is among China's most densely populated regions, with four times as many people per square mile as live in most areas of China.

With so many people, almost every spare piece of land has been built on to provide housing, some of which is very crowded.

Above: This satellite image clearly shows Chongming Island in the middle of the Yangtze just before the river reaches the East China Sea.

Housing is now spreading onto valuable farmland, creating new problems. It reduces the amount of food that can be produced.

Planners in the delta region are now turning to the skies for solutions to the delta's growing population. A vertical city has been proposed: a giant skyscraper standing 3,700 feet (1,128 meters) high and housing 100,000 people in 300 stories together with stores, offices, theaters, and hospitals.

Into the future

Our ferry leaves us in Shanghai, China's most important port, which links the Yangtze to the sea. The route into the center of the city takes us up the Huangpu river as it makes its way to join the Yangtze. We disembark at Shiliupu Wharf and from here take a stroll along the Bund, the main street on the western edge of the Huangpu. The Bund is lined with old buildings from times past when the British, French, Americans, and Japanese established trading posts in the city. Across the Huangpu is the special economic zone of Pudong MAP REF: 2 , a shining example of China's new role as a major world economy.

In 1990 Pudong was little more than farmland, but since then it has rapidly developed into a thriving business center. Covering over 39 square miles (100 square kilometres), it is an important manufacturing zone for high-tech industries such as computing and electronics. Pudong is on its way to becoming the financial center of Asia in the early 21st century.

The key to Pudong's success is Waigaoqiao Harbor, situated on the banks of the Yangtze as it enters the sea. Goods made in Pudong and other regions of China will be shipped from here throughout the world. Dredging to deepen the channel linking the Yangtze to the sea was completed in 2000 and will make it easier for larger ships to access the ports.

Shanghai and Pudong make it clear that just as the Yangtze was important in China's history, it will be of great importance to its future.

This impressive television tower dominates the landscape of the fast-growing business and industrial district of Pudong.

Journey's End

As we wait for our flight home from Pudong's international airport, opened in 1999, we can look out to the point at which the Yangtze meets the East China Sea. What an incredible journey we have had! We have experienced 3,914 miles (6,300 kilometers) of history and change, seen amazing landscapes, and shared in the daily lives of people who live by and depend on the river.

The Yangtze falls rapidly before leveling off in the second half of its 3,914-mile (6,300-kilometer) journey.

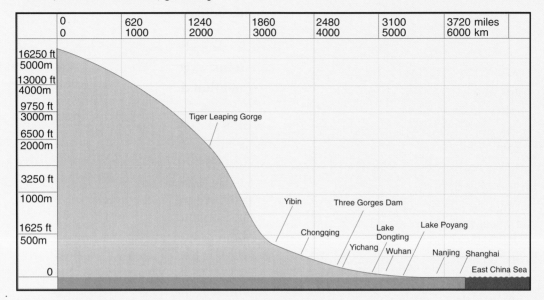

Further Information

Useful websites

http://www.pbs.org/itvs/greatwall/
This website discusses the Three Gorges Dam on the Yangtze, provides information on the river, and includes an interesting online river tour.

http://www.thewaterpage.com/yangtze.htm
This website provides a very good summary of the Yangtze and some of the issues it and its people currently face.

http://www.china-un.org/eng/5320.html
This web page provides additional information about the fascinating Naxi people and their culture and religion.

Books

Allan, Tony. *The Rise of Modern China*. Chicago: Heinemann, 2002.

Keeler, Stephen. *The Changing Face of China*. Chicago: Raintree, 2002.

Waterlow, Julia. *The Yangtze*. Milwaukee: Gareth Stevens Inc. 2003.

Glossary

bank side of a river

channel passage through which a river flows

cholera intestinal disease

commercial fish catch fish caught by the fishing industry that is then sold

confluence place where two rivers meet

current flow of water in a certain direction

dam barrier that holds or diverts water

deforestation clearing of trees from land that was once covered by forest

delta geographical feature at the mouth of a river, formed by the buildup of sediment

dike ridge built alongside a river, sea, or lake shore that holds back the water and so reduces flooding

downstream direction you travel along a river when you are moving from the source to the estuary

drainage basin area of land drained by a river and its tributaries, also known as a watershed

erosion wearing away of land by natural forces such as running water, glaciers, wind, or waves

estuary mouth of the river

faults lines of natural weakness in the earth's crust

flood rising and overflow of a river's water over its banks, onto land that is usually dry

glacier mass of snow and ice

gorge deep, narrow river valley with steep, rocky sides

headwaters water at the source of a river

hydroelectric power (HEP) electricity generated by water as it passes through turbines. HEP involves damming river valleys and forming artificial lakes.

irrigation artificial application of water to crops to make up for low or unpredictable rainfall

meander large bend in a river, usually S-shaped

meltwater water produced by the melting of snow and ice

municipality town, city, or district that has its own local government

oxbow lake small, arc-shaped lake that was once part of the former course of a river

paddy fields fields that are usually covered with shallow water, where rice is grown

peninsula narrow piece of land that juts out from the mainland into a river, lake or sea. A peninsula is surrounded by water on at least three sides.

plateau large area of land having a level surface

population density number of people living in a given area

rapids fast-moving stretches of a river

reservoir artificial lake that forms when water collects behind a dam. Reservoir water may be used for irrigation or for producing hydroelectric power.

run-off rainwater that runs off the earth's surface into rivers, streams, and lakes

sedan chair enclosed chair fixed to two poles that is carried by porters. Historically this luxury was reserved for Emperors and high nobility.

sediment fine sand and earth that is moved and deposited by water, wind, or ice

sewage waste carried by sewers for treatment or disposal. Sewage normally includes human waste and waste water, but it can include chemicals from homes, offices, and factories.

ship lock enclosed section of river, where the water level can be raised or lowered. This process helps ships move up or down the river.

shoal underwater sandbank

sluice gates gates that control the flow of water and sediment in a river channel when opened or closed

staple crops foods that form the basis of people's diets

subsistence farming farming that provides food mainly for the farmer's household. Surplus food may be sold.

terraced farming system of growing crops on horizontal steps cut into a hillside

tributary stream or river that flows into another larger stream or river

upstream direction you travel in when you are moving from the estuary back toward the source

waterfall sudden fall of water over a steep drop

waterway body of water such as a river or canal that is used as a transportation route

Index

aquaculture 34, 35

baiji (Chinese river dolphin) 36
Beijing 33, 40, 41

cargo 15, 16, 20
Chaotianmen Docks 15, 16
Chongming Island 43
Chongqing 5, 13, 14, 15, 16, 17, 18, 19, 20, 21, 24, 27, 32
cormorants 35
crops 10, 12, 35, 37, 38, 39
cruise ships 21, 22, 23, 24, 25, 28, 29

Daning River 22, 25
deforestation 11
delta 5, 34, 42, 43
Dongba 12, 13
dredging 41, 45

earthquake (Lijiang) 13, 26
East China Sea 5, 16, 20, 42, 43, 45
environment 6, 7, 11, 12, 21, 26
erosion 7, 10, 11

farmers and farming 10, 11, 30, 32, 33, 34, 35, 37, 38, 39, 43
Fengjie 14, 18, 21, 22
fish and fishing 34, 35, 36
fish farming (see aquaculture)
flooding 5, 7, 11, 14, 18, 23, 25, 26, 27, 28, 30, 31, 32, 37, 38
floodplains 29, 30

Gezhou Dam 22, 27, 28, 29
Grand Canal 34, 41

Han River 32
Huangpu River 44
hydroelectric power (HEP) 26

industries 16, 17, 20, 21, 28, 31, 33, 40, 44, 45
irrigation 37, 38

Jialing River 5, 15
Jingjiang levee 30, 31, 32

Lake Dongting 28, 32
Lesser Three Gorges 22, 25
Lijiang 5, 6, 8, 12, 13

mouth of the Yangtze 42, 43

Nanjing 5, 34, 40, 41
natural resources 16
Naxi people 12, 13

pollution 17, 21, 36
Pudong 44, 45

Qinghai-Tibet plateau 5, 6
Qutang Gorge 22–23, 25

rapids 5, 9
reservoir 18, 19, 20
rice 10, 12, 17, 34, 37, 38–39
rice paddies 34, 38, 40

Sandouping 18, 19, 22, 26
sediment 11, 23, 27, 29, 30, 32, 35, 41, 43
settlements 5, 19
Shanghai 5, 16, 41, 42, 43, 44, 45
ship locks 27, 28, 29

Szechuan basin 5, 13, 14
Szechuan hotpot 17
source of the Yangtze 7
Sun Yat-sen 40

textiles 28, 32–33
Three Gorges Dam 5, 18, 20, 21, 22, 23, 24, 25, 26, 27, 29
Tiger Leaping Gorge 6, 8–9, 10
tourism 8, 12, 13, 21, 22, 24, 25, 29, 40
trade 14, 20, 42, 44
transportation 15, 16, 20, 29, 32–33, 41
tributaries 5, 23, 32, 37

upper Yangtze 7, 8, 12, 21, 31

waste 21, 35
wildlife 34, 36
Wu Gorge 25
Wuhan 24, 28, 31, 32, 33, 34
Wushan 22, 25

Xiling Gorge 23, 25, 26

Yibin 5, 13
Yichang 5, 20, 22, 28, 29

Zhenjiang 34, 41